D0116043

KILLER ANIMALS
SCORPIONS
ON THE HUNT

by Janet Riehecky

Reading Consultant:
Barbara J. Fox
Reading Specialist
North Carolina State University

Content Consultant:
Lorenzo Prendini, PhD
Associate Curator: Arachnids and Myriapods
Division of Invertebrate Zoology
American Museum of Natural History
New York, New York

Capstone
press

Mankato, Minnesota

Blazers is published by Capstone Press,
151 Good Counsel Drive, P.O. Box 669, Mankato, Minnesota 56002.
www.capstonepress.com

Books published by Capstone Press are manufactured with paper
containing at least 10 percent post-consumer waste.

Library of Congress Cataloging-in-Publication Data
Riehecky, Janet, 1953–
    Scorpions : on the hunt / by Janet Riehecky.
    p. cm. — (Blazers. Killer animals)
    Includes bibliographical references and index.
    Summary: "Describes scorpions, their physical features, how they hunt and kill,
and their role in the ecosystem" — Provided by publisher.
    ISBN 978-1-4296-3388-8 (library binding)
    1. Scorpions — Juvenile literature. I. Title.
QL458.7.R54 2010
595.4'6 — dc22   2009000651

Editorial Credits
Abby Czeskleba, editor; Bobbi J. Wyss, book designer; Kyle Grenz, set designer;
    Svetlana Zhurkin, media researcher

Photo Credits
DigitalVision, 11, 22–23
Minden Pictures/Michael & Patricia Fogden, 20–21
Nature Picture Library/Barry Mansell, 6–7; Premaphotos, 16
Peter Arnold/Biosphoto/Christophe Véchot, 28–29; Daniel Heuclin, 14–15; Laurent Conchon, 13
Photoshot/Bruce Coleman/J.C. Carton, 18–19, 24–25; John Bell, 4–5
Shutterstock/EcoPrint, 8; Sebastian Duda, cover, 26–27

TABLE OF CONTENTS

A HIDE-AND-WAIT KILLER

A hungry scorpion waits for **prey** to come near. Soon the scorpion feels the air move. A beetle walks nearby. It doesn't see the scorpion.

prey – an animal hunted by another animal for food

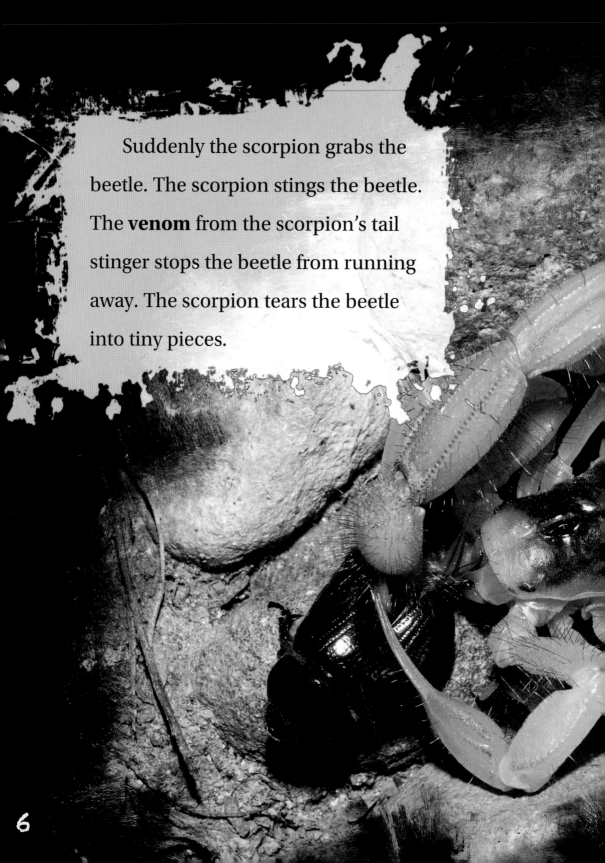

Suddenly the scorpion grabs the beetle. The scorpion stings the beetle. The **venom** from the scorpion's tail stinger stops the beetle from running away. The scorpion tears the beetle into tiny pieces.

venom – poisonous liquid produced by
some animals

SMALL BUT DANGEROUS

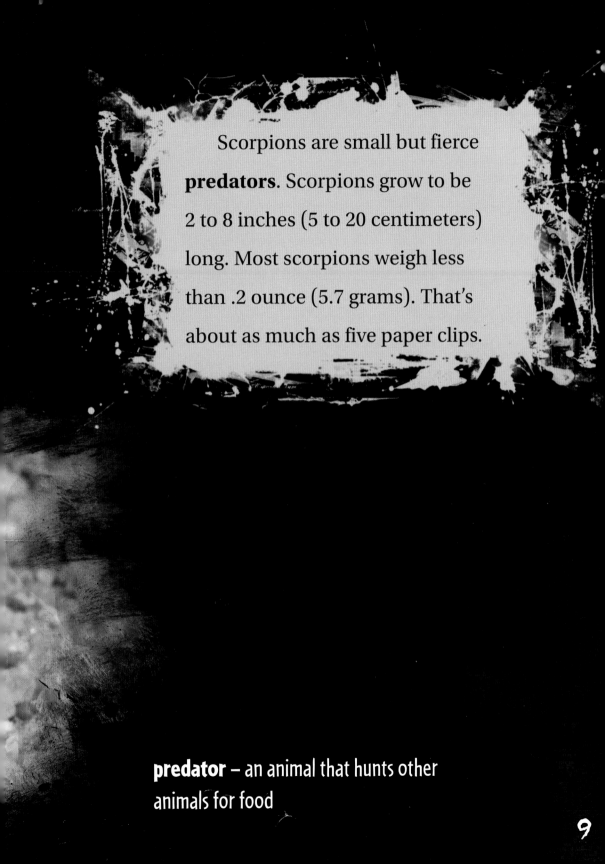

Scorpions are small but fierce **predators**. Scorpions grow to be 2 to 8 inches (5 to 20 centimeters) long. Most scorpions weigh less than .2 ounce (5.7 grams). That's about as much as five paper clips.

predator – an animal that hunts other animals for food

Scorpions have an easy time finding food. Small body hairs help them feel the air move. These hairs also feel the ground move when prey walks nearby.

KILLER FACT

Scorpions have up to 12 eyes, but they can't see very well.

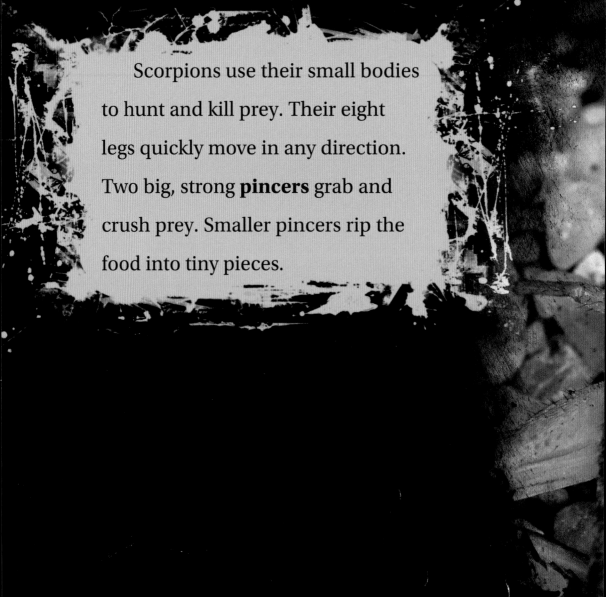

Scorpions use their small bodies to hunt and kill prey. Their eight legs quickly move in any direction. Two big, strong **pincers** grab and crush prey. Smaller pincers rip the food into tiny pieces.

pincer – a claw used to hold prey

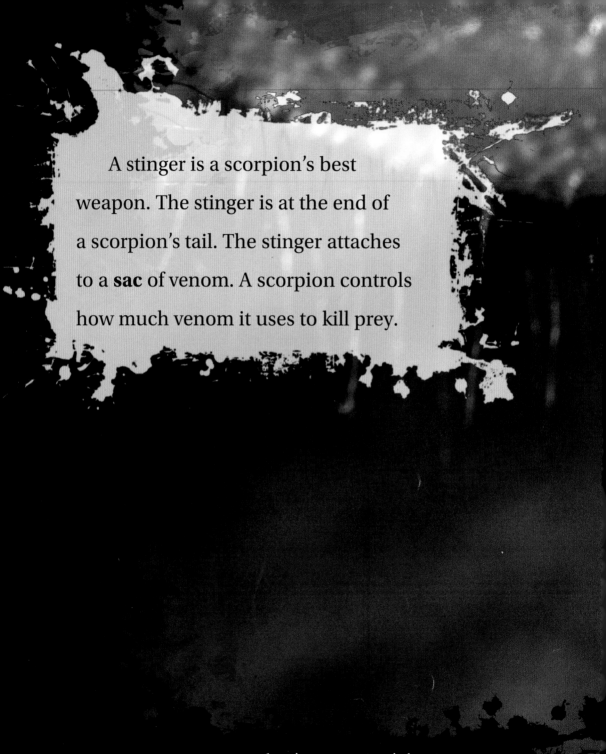

A stinger is a scorpion's best weapon. The stinger is at the end of a scorpion's tail. The stinger attaches to a **sac** of venom. A scorpion controls how much venom it uses to kill prey.

sac – a part of a plant or animal that is shaped like a pocket or bag

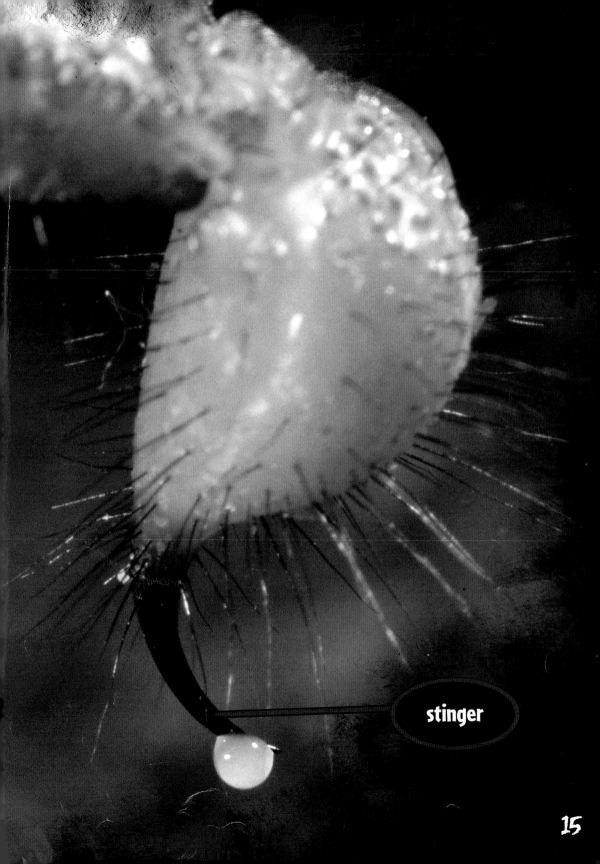

stinger

15

A DEADLY HUNTER

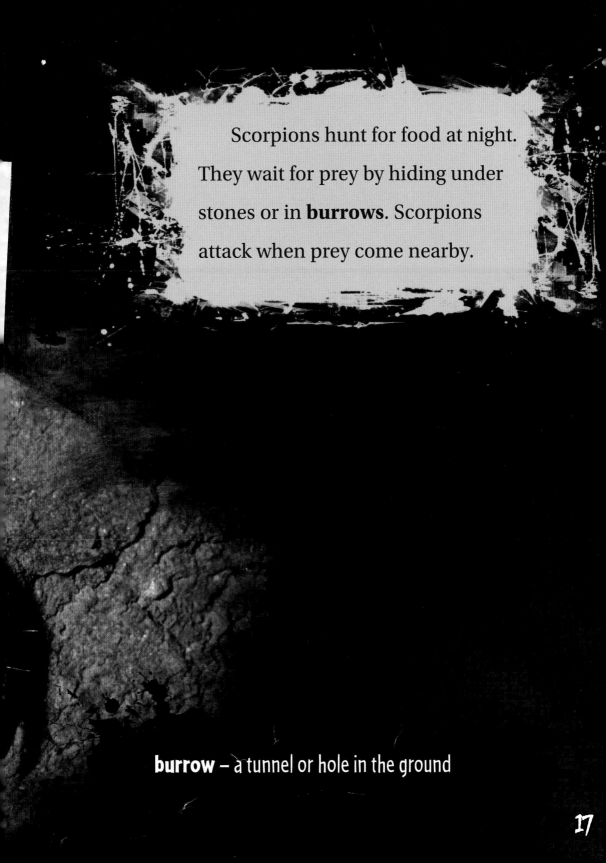

Scorpions hunt for food at night. They wait for prey by hiding under stones or in **burrows**. Scorpions attack when prey come nearby.

burrow – a tunnel or hole in the ground

KILLER FACT

Scorpions can feel prey walking as far as 3 feet (1 meter) away.

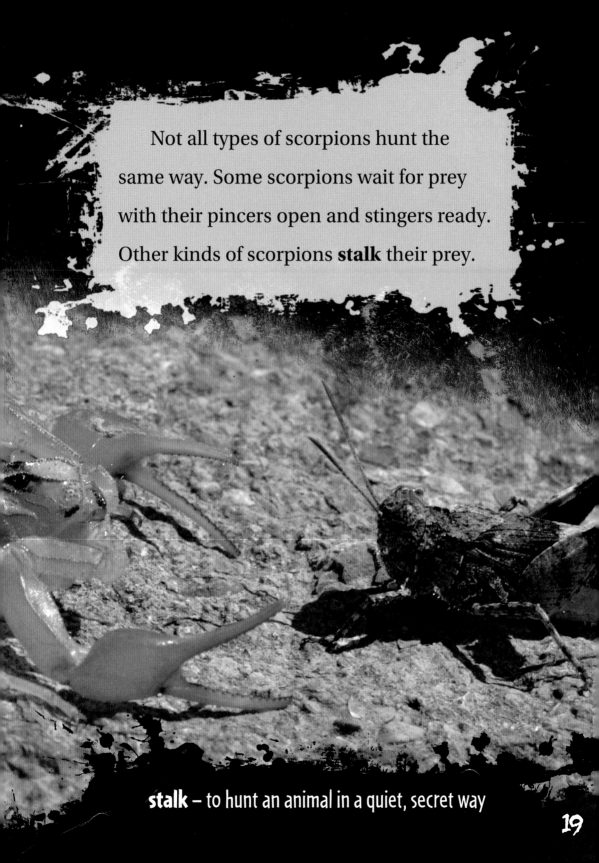

Not all types of scorpions hunt the same way. Some scorpions wait for prey with their pincers open and stingers ready. Other kinds of scorpions **stalk** their prey.

stalk – to hunt an animal in a quiet, secret way

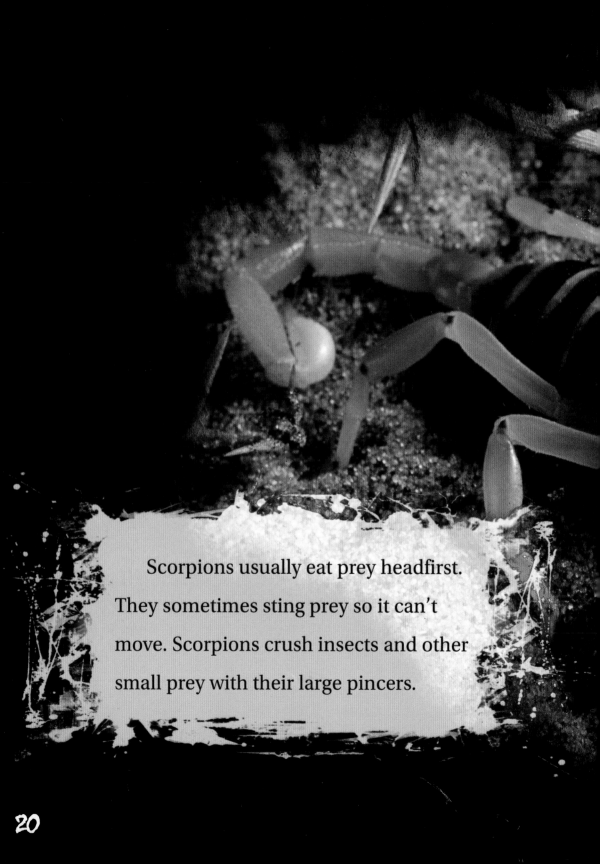

Scorpions usually eat prey headfirst. They sometimes sting prey so it can't move. Scorpions crush insects and other small prey with their large pincers.

Scorpion Diagram

venom sac

stinger

tail

leg

pincer

HELPING THE ECOSYSTEM

Scorpions play an important part in the **ecosystem**. They eat insects, worms, spiders, and small lizards. Scorpions lower the number of insects and small animals. Too many animals can be bad for the ecosystem.

ecosystem – a group of animals and plants that work together with their surroundings

Scorpions sting people when they sense danger. Some scorpion stings can kill people. But most scorpions cannot hurt humans. People must respect these small but deadly predators.

KILLER FACT

There are more than 1,500 types of scorpions. Fewer than 30 kinds of scorpions are dangerous to humans.

Making the Kill!

29

GLOSSARY

attach (uh-TACH) — to join something

burrow (BUR-oh) — a tunnel or hole in the ground

ecosystem (EE-koh-sis-tuhm) — a group of animals and plants that work together with their surroundings

pincer (PIN-sur) — a claw used to hold prey

predator (PRED-uh-tur) — an animal that hunts other animals for food

prey (PRAY) — an animal hunted by another animal for food

sac (SAK) — a part of a plant or animal that is shaped like a pocket or bag

stalk (STAWK) — to hunt an animal in a quiet, secret way

venom (VEN-uhm) — poisonous liquid produced by some animals

Read More

McFee, Shane. *Scorpions*. Poison! New York: PowerKids Press, 2008.

Murray, Peter. *Scorpions*. New Naturebooks. Mankato, Minn.: Child's World, 2008.

Thomas, Isabel. *Scorpion vs. Tarantula*. Animals Head to Head. Chicago: Raintree, 2006.

Internet Sites

FactHound offers a safe, fun way to find Internet sites related to this book. All of the sites on FactHound have been researched by our staff.

Here's all you do:

Visit *www.facthound.com*

FactHound will fetch the best sites for you!

INDEX